Celebrate Easter

A Christian Coloring book

Copyright © 2021 Hearth Write Press

All rights reserved. This book or any portion thereof may not be reproduced or used in any manner whatsoever without the express written permission of the publisher except for the use of brief quotations in a book review.

Published by Hearth Write Press

307 E 4th Street

Bird City, KS 67731

Cover and interior design by DM Burns

All images sourced from Creative Fabrica.

Test Page

Use the icons below to test your tools before you begin coloring. You can try with markers, watercolors, glitter pens, whatever inspires you. Remember to check for bleed through on the back of the page. Happy coloring!

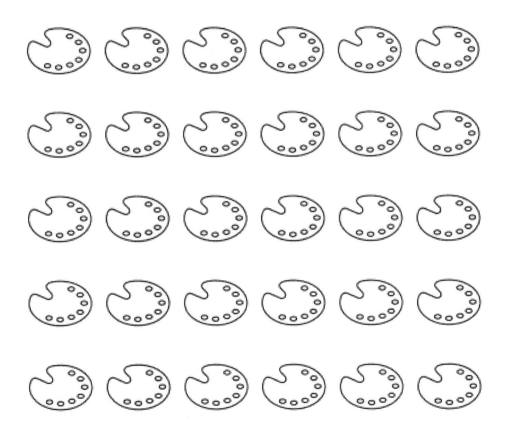

Test Page

Use the icons below to test your tools before you begin coloring. You can try with markers, watercolors, glitter pens, whatever inspires you. Remember to check for bleed through on the back of the page. Happy coloring!

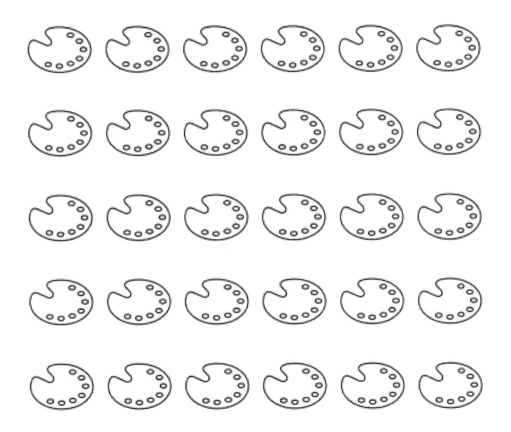

Blessed ARE THOSE WHO HAVE NOT seen AND YET HAVE Believed

Jesus Before Jelly Beans

FOR God SO LOVED THE
WORLD
THAT HE GAVE ONLY BEGOTTEN
Son

I KNOW THAT MY REDEEMER Lives

FORGET THE EGGS
I ALREADY FOUND
Jesus

It's not about the bunny about it's the lamb

But the greatest of these is

faith　*love*　*hope*

He is not here for he is risen as he said come see the place where the Lord laid

Passion Week Scripture Reading

Day 1 (Palm Sunday) Matthew 21:1-11

Day 2 Read Matthew 21: 12-20

Day 3 Read Matthew 21: 20-27

Day 4 Read Luke 22:1-6 and Mark 14: 1-11

Day 5 (Last Supper) Read John 19:1-18 and Isaiah 54:7

Day 6 (Good Friday) Read Mark 14:53-15:41

   Read Isaiah 53:5-6

   Read 1 Peter 1:18-21

Day 7 Read John 19:38-42 and Romans 6:22-23

Day 8   **The Resurrection**

   Read Mark 16:1-7

   And

   Matthew 28: 1-20

Copyright © 2021 Hearth Write Press

All rights reserved. This book or any portion thereof may not be reproduced or used in any manner whatsoever without the express written permission of the publisher except for the use of brief quotations in a book review.

Published by Hearth Write Press

307 E 4th Street

Bird City, KS 67731

Cover and interior design by DM Burns

All images sourced from Creative Fabrica.

CPSIA information can be obtained
at www.ICGtesting.com
Printed in the USA
LVHW061204190323
741971LV00024B/628